Mumps

Story by Beverley Randell

Illustrated by Ernest Papps

On Monday

Tom came home after school
and said,
"I'm not hungry.
I'm going to bed."

On Tuesday

"Mom! Mom, come here!"
said Tom.

"Mumps," said Mom.
"Stay in bed
and we will take care of you."

Dad came in.

"Mumps," he said.

"You look like this!

Stay in bed, Tom."

Mom and Dad
took care of Tom.

He stayed in bed
and he went to sleep.

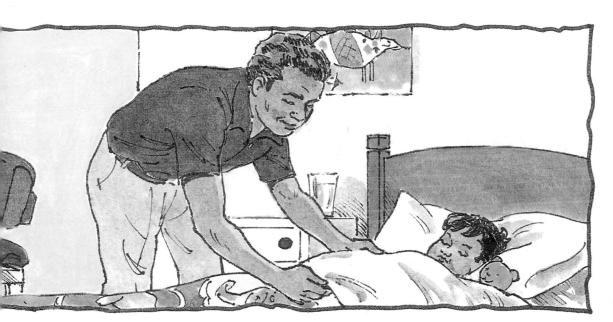

On Wednesday

Dad said,
"Here you are, Tom.
This is a book
for you to read."

On Thursday

Tom said, "Look at me!
My mumps are going down."

On Friday

"I'm hungry," said Tom.

"Where are the mumps?"
said Mom.

"They went away," said Tom.